GREAT PIANO TRIOS

Joseph Haydn

DOVER PUBLICATIONS, INC.
New York

Bibliographical Note

This Dover edition, first published in 1995, is a new compilation of twelve unabridged works
taken from *Trios für Pianoforte, Violine u. Violoncell von Joseph Haydn, revidiert von Fr[iedrich]
Hermann,* Band I and Band II, originally published by C. F. Peters, Leipzig, n.d. The Dover edition
adds: a list of contents; a preface drawn from Charles Rosen's *The Classical Style* (W. W. Norton &
Company, New York, 1972); publisher's notes; and new headings and movement numbers
throughout.

The publisher is grateful to the following individuals and organizations for their kind help in
making this edition possible: Tim Cherubini, Duke University Music Library; violinist Isidore
Cohen, former member of the Beaux Arts Trio; violinist Robert Mann, the Juilliard School and the
Juilliard String Quartet; Joseph Schwartz, Professor of Piano and member of the Oberlin Piano
Trio, Oberlin College Conservatory of Music; and to W. W. Norton & Company for their generous
permission to reprint excerpts from Charles Rosen's book.

Library of Congress Cataloging-in-Publication Data

Haydn, Joseph, 1732–1809.
[Trios, piano, strings. Selections]
Great piano trios / Joseph Haydn.
1 score.
Originally published (new compilation): Trios für Pianoforte, Violine u. Violoncell / von
Joseph Haydn ; revidiert von Fr. Hermann. Leipzig : C. F. Peters, 18—. Bd. 1–2. With new
introd.
Contents: E minor, Hob. XV, no. 12 — A-flat major, Hob. XV, no. 14 — A major, Hob. XV,
no. 18 — D minor, Hob. XV, no. 23 — D major, Hob. XV, no. 24 — G major, Hob. XV, no. 25 —
F-sharp minor, Hob. XV, no. 26 — C major, Hob. XV, no. 27 — E major, Hob. XV, no. 28 —
E-flat major, Hob. XV, no. 29 — E-flat major, Hob. XV, no. 30 — E-flat minor, Hob. XV, no. 31.
ISBN 0-486-28728-9
1. Piano trios—Scores. I. Title.
M312.H43G7   1995   95-17329
                                                        CIP
                                                        M

Manufactured in the United States of America
Dover Publications, Inc., 31 East 2nd Street, Mineola, N.Y. 11501

CONTENTS

*Hoboken: Poco Adagio. Cantabile
**The heading "Finale" does not appear in Hoboken's listing.

PREFACE

The fact that these trios are essentially solo works makes possible their greatest quality, a feeling of improvisation almost unique in Haydn's work, and, indeed, rarely found in any of the three great [C]lassic composers. Haydn was a composer who needed the piano in order to write music; these trios seem to give us Haydn at work. They have a spontaneous quality that the composer rarely sought elsewhere; their inspiration seems relaxed and unforced, at times almost disorganized, when compared with the quartets and symphonies. The forms are also more relaxed: a great many of the trios have dance finales—minuets or German peasant dances—and some of the first movements are among Haydn's finest double-variation sets. . . .

Haydn's imagination is particularly luxuriant in these trios. Unconstrained by considerations of public effect, as in the symphonies, or by impressive refinements of style as in the quartets, Haydn wrote them for the sheer pleasure of the solo instrumentalists.

CHARLES ROSEN, *The Classical Style**

*W. W. Norton & Company, New York, 1972: pp. 352, 354. By permission.

PUBLISHER'S NOTES

NUMBERING THE PIANO TRIOS

The Dover edition of twelve piano trios by Joseph Haydn follows the catalog numbers established by bibliographer Anthony van Hoboken's *Joseph Haydn: Thematisch-bibliographisches Werkverzeichnis* (1957–71) in the section designated "Gruppe XV: Trios für Klavier, Violine (oder Flöte) und Violoncello."

The scores, however, are reprinted from an edition that established a different numbering sequence throughout three volumes: *Trios für Pianoforte, Violine u[nd] Violoncell von Joseph Haydn, revidiert* [supervised] *von Fr. Hermann,* published by C. F. Peters, Leipzig, n.d.

The Hoboken and Peters numbers are matched as follows:

From Group XV	Peters Edition		
Hob. No. 12 [Em]	Vol. I,	Trio	VII
" " 11 [A-flat]	" I,	"	XI
" " 18 [A]	" II,	"	XIII
" " 23 [Dm]	" II,	"	XXIII
" " 24 [D]	" I,	"	VI
" " 25 [G]	" I,	"	I
" " 26 [F-sharp m] . . .	" I,	"	II
" " 27 [C]	" I,	"	III
" " 28 [E]	" I,	"	IV
" " 29 [E-flat]	" I,	"	V
" " 30 [E-flat]	" I,	"	VIII
" " 31 [E-flat m]	" II,	"	XVIII

HAYDN'S DEDICATIONS

Haydn's dedications of his piano trios are as follows, according to Hoboken and Rosen (see Preface). Further information about the Esterházys is based on *Grove*'s* article about the composer's Hungarian patrons.

PIANO TRIO XV:18 [also Nos. 19 and 20, omitted in this edition] is dedicated to the Princess Maria Anna Esterházy, formerly Countess Hohenfeld, wife of Prince Anton.

PIANO TRIO XV:23 [also Nos. 21 and 22, omitted here] is dedicated to the Princess Maria (Josepha) Esterházy, formerly Princess of Liechtenstein, wife of Prince Nikolaus.

PIANO TRIOS XV:24–26 are dedicated to Rebecca Schroeter, a young English widow who served as Haydn's copyist in London.

PIANO TRIOS XV:27–29 are dedicated to Madame Theresa (Jansen) Bartolozzi, wife of the engraver Francesco Bartolozzi.

There is no indication of any dedication for Piano Trios XV:12, 14, 30 or 31.

The New Grove Dictionary of Music and Musicians, Vol. 6, Macmillan, London, 1980.

PIANO TRIO IN E MINOR
Hob. XV: No. 12

I.

(before 1789)

Piano Trio in E Minor [Hob. XV: 12]

Piano Trio in E Minor [Hob. XV: 12]

II.

III.

Rondo.
Presto.

Piano Trio in E Minor [Hob. XV: 12]

Piano Trio in E Minor [Hob. XV: 12]

PIANO TRIO IN A-FLAT MAJOR
Hob. XV: No. 14
I.

Piano Trio in A-flat Major [Hob. XV: 14]

Piano Trio in A-flat Major [Hob. XV: 14]

Piano Trio in A-flat Major [Hob. XV: 14]

Piano Trio in A-flat Major [Hob. XV: 14]

II.

Piano Trio in A-flat Major [Hob. XV: 14]

III.

Piano Trio in A-flat Major [Hob. XV: 14]

PIANO TRIO IN A MAJOR
Hob. XV: No. 18

I.

(no later than 1794)

II.

III.

Piano Trio in A Major [Hob. XV: 18]

PIANO TRIO IN D MINOR

Hob. XV: No. 23

I.

(1794–5)

II.

Finale III.

Vivace.

Vivace.

Piano Trio in D Minor [Hob. XV: 23]

PIANO TRIO IN D MAJOR
Hob. XV: No. 24

I.

(no later than 1795)

Piano Trio in D Major [Hob. XV: 24]

Piano Trio in D Major [Hob. XV: 24]

II.

attacca:

III.

PIANO TRIO IN G MAJOR
Hob. XV: No. 25
I.

(no later than 1795)

Piano Trio in G Major [Hob. XV: 25]

II.

Poco Adagio.

III.

Finale.
Rondo all' Ongarese.
Presto.

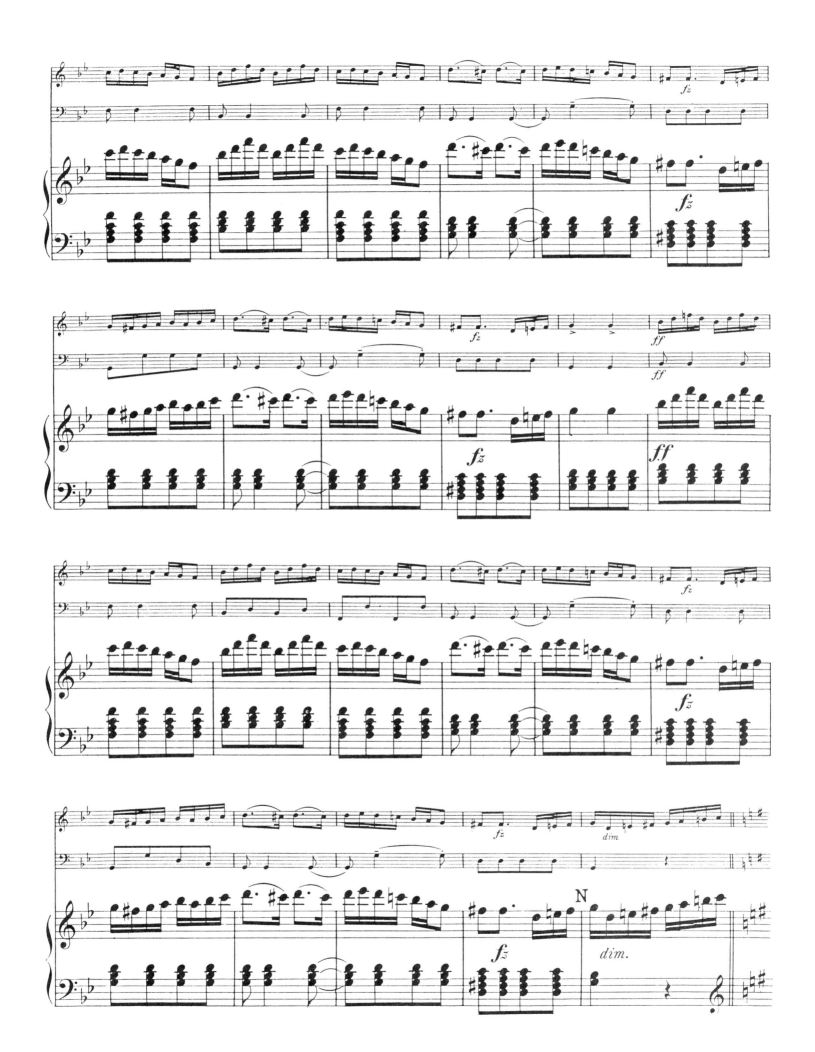

Maggiore.

PIANO TRIO IN F-SHARP MINOR
Hob. XV: No. 26
I.

(no later than 1795)

Piano Trio in F-sharp Minor [Hob. XV: 26]

II.

Piano Trio in F-sharp Minor [Hob. XV: 26] 129

Piano Trio in F-sharp Minor [Hob. XV: 26]

III.

Finale.
Tempo di Menuetto.

Tempo di Menuetto.

PIANO TRIO IN C MAJOR
Hob. XV: No. 27

I.

(before 1797)

Piano Trio in C Major [Hob. XV: 27]

Piano Trio in C Major [Hob. XV: 27]

Piano Trio in C Major [Hob. XV: 27]

Piano Trio in C Major [Hob. XV: 27]

PIANO TRIO IN E MAJOR
Hob. XV: No. 28
I.

(before 1797)

Piano Trio in E Major [Hob. XV: 28]

II.

Piano Trio in E Major [Hob. XV: 28]

III.

Finale.
Allegro.

Piano Trio in E Major [Hob. XV: 28]

PIANO TRIO IN E-FLAT MAJOR
Hob. XV: No. 29

I.

(before 1797)

II.

Finale.
Allemande.
Presto assai.

Presto assai.

Piano Trio in E-flat Major [Hob. XV: 29]

Piano Trio in E-flat Major [Hob. XV: 29]

PIANO TRIO IN E-FLAT MAJOR
Hob. XV: No. 30

I.

(1795)

Piano Trio in E-flat Major [Hob. XV: 30]

II.

III.

Piano Trio in E-flat Major [Hob. XV: 30]

Piano Trio in E-flat Major [Hob. XV: 30]

PIANO TRIO IN E-FLAT MINOR
Hob. XV: No. 31

Andante cantabile. **I.**

(1795)

Piano Trio in E-flat Minor [Hob. XV: 31]

II.

Piano Trio in E-flat Minor [Hob. XV: 31]

Piano Trio in E-flat Minor [Hob. XV: 31]

END OF EDITION